Alone
with
Love Songs

Also By Edwin Romond

Dream Teaching

Home Fire

Macaroons (chapbook)

Blue Mountain Time: Selected Poems about Baseball (chapbook)

Alone
with
Love Songs

Edwin Romond

Grayson Books

West Hartford, Connecticut

Published by Grayson Books
West Hartford, Connecticut

Printed in the USA

www.graysonbooks.com

Romond, Edwin.
Alone with love songs / Edwin Romond.
p. cm.
Poems.
ISBN-13: 978-0-9785382-8-6
ISBN-10: 0-9785382-8-5

I. Title.

PS3618.O655A46 2011   811'.6
                      QBI11-600055

ISBN: 978-0-9785382-8-6

Book Design by Virginia Anstett

For
Penny Schickling
my sister

Contents

I. Songs

II. Snakes

III. Shifting Gears

I

Songs

Alone with Love Songs

It was an old motel
overlooking
Lake Michigan
the rooms converted
to tiny furnished
apartments
for people like me,
single, straight
out of Catholic seminary,
for $85 a month
just enough space
to live for the first time
by myself.
Some days
I'd stand for hours
gazing out at waves
sipping coffee and
smoking the cigarettes
I needed like air,
not the last time
in my life
I would crave
what was killing me.
And I'd listen to records
long past memorizing
and in the company
of solitude
I fell in love
with love songs.
Years before mortgages
and picking out patio furniture
I shared my time
with Sinatra and Mathis,
Linda Ronstadt,
and Carole King, just music
and me, my eyes set

on restless Lake Michigan
vast as the future when
you're 20 and in love
with the promise of love
from James Taylor
or Joni Mitchell.
When Wisconsin snow
would erase the lake
from my window
I'd feel a blizzard of flames
inside me as I listened
deeply hour after hour
to haunting ballads blurring
distance between the romantic
and the real, and I,
love's lonely apprentice,
taking it all in,
getting it all wrong.

Decembers

Snow would wiggle
beneath our streetlights
when each December
seemed a miracle. I loved
snapping the kitchen shade
to find Albert Street icing
white. I loved hurrying
my homework to walk
with my brother and our dog
across the turnpike overpass
where miles of brake lights
and jingling tire chains
made us wish for Christmas.
Our collie would grow
a slush beard as our words
turned to steam, then faded
as fast as the foot and paw prints
we'd leave back to our house
that looked like a gift
wrapped in white around
the porch light burning gold
into the streams of falling snow.

Johnny Cash

His voice swears
he lives somewhere
between condemnation
and redemption and
was there ever such a man
who could sing
about love and murder
and make you trust
him with your soul?
No man's voice is dark
as a shadow in a coal mine
without having lost
almost everything
and earned the life
to tell about it
in songs of freight trains
and prisons, death,
and addiction, women
who broke him
and the one who made
him whole. You know
he's made friends
with Jesus but
Satan's never far away
and you love this man
whose face is etched
in nightmares, but whose eyes
see past eternity's door
as he stands in black,
growling songs of regret
and gratitude, teaching
your heart how to die and live.

My Request of Yankee Stadium's Demolition Workers

Please have one more cup of coffee
before you start your labor.
All I ask is a moment
to place my ear to the outside wall
like a seashell from time's ocean.
Let me hear my father's voice
that October day in 1960, my first time
in this cathedral. Let me touch
this concrete like a tombstone and
hold the gold memory of his love
up in section 36. Let me say
goodbye with my hands and heart
before you crush it all to dust.

My Mother at 20

Running to the station
from her Rahway, NJ house leaving
her parents, her six brothers and sisters,
leaving the dogs and chickens
in the backyard, running all the way
to the train for downtown
1929 Newark, vital, noisy
with people from street to street.
And my mother, 20, on the train
smiling at the conductor,
happy and alert, riding tracks
to Newark's Penn Station filled
with squeals of rail cars bringing
mostly men to work. Margaret Brennan,
my mother, tall, lean, movie star beautiful,
her wide brimmed hat flapping,
dashing to the Prudential building
up the stairs to her place among men.
Career woman before career women
she thrives in the busyness of business,
the morning speeding by like youth.
Then, out to lunch, quick shopping
on Market and Broad Streets
before racing back to Prudential
and the IBM keyboard she wields
with the grace of a pianist.
5 o'clock sends her running again
for a train to Asbury Park
where my future father has driven his truck
to swim with her in the day's last gold.
The two of them close in salty foam,
young, in love, their life together a book
just beginning. Then waltzing under stars
to the band on the boardwalk, dancing
every dance and after the last dance
a truck ride home to Rahway

where she races to her room
to sleep with the dreams of a woman happy
with her life while miles of train tracks
north, Newark waits for morning and
my mother at 20, who will wake
to see good work, sweet love, and full life
all in front of her and run as fast as she can.

Almost Forever

He is 14, filled with the flames of young love
so he writes a poem for the literary magazine titled,
"Forever: for Susan," and sweetens the lines
with *always, eternal, unending,* and *everlasting,*
extremities of first romance that made me smile.
And who could not be moved by his earnest vow
in the last verse, *As long as there is a golden sun,*
you, dear love, are my only one? But this morning
he rushes to my room, face flushed, breathless,
and asks, "Did the book go to press yet?"
When I say, "No" his voice fills with fire as he begs
for his poem back. I pull "Forever: for Susan"
from the folder, and watch him take a thick eraser
to rub out *Susan* and write in, *Tiffany,* before
racing back to the crowded hall. There are still
six minutes until homeroom, almost forever
for a boy with a love poem, a hunter's eyes,
and a stiff eraser bulging his blue jeans.

To My Neighbor

That night last week when our block lost power
you and I stood outside with flashlights and joked
about what still could be done in the dark.
I was lying to you, Joe; I wasn't really thinking
about sex. I was wondering if I could use this
in a poem. Before you suddenly have somewhere
else to go, may I tell you that some nights
I've seen you out back wrestling with your sons
and I've thought how you could write about the feel
of each other's arms, each other's breath,
and record the joy of tumbling in grass.
I write poems, Joe; I don't hunt deer as you do
although there's lots about an October forest
and talking in whispers with your buddies
that could make a page beautiful. Joe, I'm a poet,
and also a thief, because that night we lost electric
you said, "It takes the dark to appreciate the moon"
and I stole that for some lines about the power
of friendship. Stop by sometime for a beer
and a poem with your words lighting the first verse.

After 11 Years

She could tell him that their porch air
smelled last night like autumn
and through the shedding trees
she saw birds flying only in circles.
When he took her hand and his voice rose
speaking of re-mortgaging and low interest,
she could tell him she was thinking of old films,
how she watches them knowing nothing
new can happen. And when he spoke
of fixed rates and 15 years and 30 years,
she could only hear the traffic, other
lives going north and south, other wives
locked in seat belts next to husbands,
watching the repetition of broken lines
and wishing for more than more of the same.
What she couldn't tell him was why
later she undressed in the bathroom,
or why she tied herself in a bathrobe
then turned away from him into the blue
light of the alarm clock to watch its hands
crawl around and around as he snored.

Green

It was the color of our shingles,
my father's tool box, and the bench
I stayed on in Little League.
For one of life's kinder contradictions
it's the tint of my blackboards, for one
of its cruelties, it's the first hue to leave
our poplars in September. I favor it in eyes
and beer bottles, it's the only peace I find
in army camouflage. My wife wore it
on our first date, I wore it when I proposed.
Once it was the name of the street where we lived.
I've never told anyone I think it's beautiful
in front of gravestones. I love its spray
from my lawn mower on summer mornings
and the needles of our Christmas tree crushed
through a doorway. It's the color of the mug
I pour tea in after bad classes and the tie
I knot the next morning for a fresh start.
Even Death could be okay if I can take green
with me and, if God's a good guy, He'll let me
wing around forever with an eternity of green
to land in whenever I feel like living.

Musical Soul

for Alfred Minicozzi

Bali Ha'i may call you, any night any day.
In your heart you'll hear it call you: "Come away … Come away."

I could hear the choral director
in the room across the hall
from where I lay in a bunk bed
with a sore throat and fever.
No boarding school classes for me that day,
just hours and hours of dormitory silence.
But after supper his voice at glee club
rehearsal was a welcome sound
introducing a song from *South Pacific*
called "Bali Ha'i." "Close your eyes,"
he told them, "picture an exotic island,
palm trees, immaculate sand,
succulent fruit, foamy waves and
a sea breeze warmed by tropical sun,
a place where life is wonderful
in ways you've never known before."
And then the first sounds
of teenage tenor and bass voices
floating across the hall to my bunk
as he urged them, "Put your *hearts*
into it, boys! Let the audience see it!
Let them *taste* that salty air!"
And I, his secret listener in the dark,
felt the singing lift me
from the loneliness of the dorm
to the enchantment of a mystical island.
This man led the haunting call
to *come away … come away*
and his musical soul made my bunk
a magic carpet carrying me off
into the nighttime sky
on Pacific Ocean winds.

February Blizzard

I've found this picture
I thought I had thrown away and,
as snow slams my windows,
she grins beside a Vermont pond,
a jeweled waterfall from her hands,
her hair blonde over bare shoulders warm
with the gold of summer. In her eyes
a blue promise of always.

Cruel how time can turn
photos into lies and make joy
the first chapter of despair.
In the fireplace I watch her bend
toward me then turn to cinder.
I pour another glass of wine.
I toss a second log into her flame.
It will be cold tonight.

For the Movie of My Life
I Audition Former Lovers
for the Part of Muse

I'd consider Susan, but she only proved
how dull surrender can be and I tired
of her phone calls later that made lying
as exhausting as sex with a saint.
There's Amanda, but her inspiration
was baggage from the past, the ruins
of life lived in flashback: the father
she hated, the affairs with professors,
too many names and the endings the same.
Joanie just glares so she'll never do,
all her anger from Milwaukee would kill
my poems before they hit the page.
Vegan Samantha promises odes to broccoli
and squash so I guess my muse is Cassie,
whose eyes flamed with invitation and anguish,
who'd say "tomorrow" and mean "someday,"
who'd promise to call then send a postcard,
who swore that sex with me was so good
she actually thought of her first husband.
I say, "You get the part," but she sighs,
"I may or may not want it. Call me tonight.
Leave a message. Sometimes my machine is off
but you can keep trying."

New York City, circa 1980

If ever you open an album
of old vacation photos and

find a stranger grinning
behind your family

perhaps it was I
when I hungered

for something tender
so I joined you and

those you loved and,
on the count of three,

smiled with all of you
as if I actually belonged.

II

Snakes

Driving Home
from Knoebels Amusement Park

All day my five year old son has lived
through amusement park rides of make-believe
danger and now, in the real world of Route 80,
he sleeps in the back strapped in his booster seat
as traffic whizzes past. He is clutching
his giant souvenir pencil so large and thick
he could write his whole life story with it
and it's his life I think about as I maneuver
our car up and down the Pennsylvania mountain
highway where almost no one is obeying the law.
This is his world beyond rides he rode today
screaming with laughter, this is reality after
crashing bumper cars and the "Suicide
Water Slide." And I am seized with true fear
when that driver with one hand on a cell phone
swerves into my lane but my son sleeps on
holding his pencil like a scepter, maybe dreaming
of his hilarious terror aboard the "Cyclone"
and the "Anaconda" roller coaster where fright
is what you pay for and safety is assured.
When a woman speeds past applying lip stick
I grip the wheel tighter knowing I drive
with Liam's life in my hands here on Route 80
where no one cares for him as much as I do
and I am stiff with his absolute faith
that lets him doze even now as a tractor trailer,
30 miles over the speed limit, catches up
to our bumper and high beams us out of its way.
As I change lanes and it barges past like a bully,
I shudder to think the unthinkable for my son
who giggled through the "Chamber of Death"
fun house, who now sleeps trusting me
to steer clear of every horror around him.

Divorced Parents
at a Little League Game

They arrive in separate cars.
They sit on separate sides.
They cheer for #10,
the boy
they both call son.
They shout his name
across the diamond
their voices merging
like breath of spouses
making love and
he turns to left field
to wave to mom;
turns to right field
to wave to dad.
Two people
who love him;
he'll go home
with only one.

Night Watchmen

They labor beneath the burden of nothing
to do, the exhaustion nothing assumes
when left with the quiet

of deserted halls, where each squeak might
mean a blade or bullet to make true
the nightmare of those who guard in the dark.

They pass windows smeared like blackboards
with chalky streetlight and consider other
men who live this time in shadowy rooms

sleeping with women beneath the moon,
sky's night light for the rest of the world,
safe in the embrace of blankets and dreams.

Instead, night watchmen feel the solace
of coffee at 3 a.m. in the company
of a thermos holding black energy

to widen their eyes in the empty hours
as they chart the hushed regions of night
and wait, like Eskimos, for the tip of the sun.

At the George W. Bush
Iraq War Room of Empty Chairs

"In his final word, the CIA's top weapons inspector
in Iraq said Monday that the hunt for
weapons of mass destruction has
'gone as far as feasible' and has found nothing."
Associated Press, April 25, 2005

"4,287 American soldiers have been killed
in the Iraq War."
Global Security.org December 13, 2010

"Every name (of a deceased soldier) is a lightning stroke
to some heart and breaks like thunder
over some home ..."
From an 1863 Gettysburg newspaper
four days after the battle

Right this way
to the Thanksgiving table exhibit.
See the empty seat shadow
faces of a family trying to remember
what it is to be grateful.
And you baseball fans, slide into the vacant
spot in the bleachers, imagine a son
in center field looking over to see
his mother and finding no one.
And there's more! The empty chairs
at birthday parties, graduations,
kitchen table at breakfast empty chairs,
front porch on summer evening empty chairs,
and empty chairs next to kids
needing help with their homework.
And don't miss our Christmas Eve display
of children with dead eyes
at the most wonderful time of the year.
Watch their widowed mother stare
at the empty sofa when Sinatra sings
"I'll Be Home For Christmas."
If it gets too crowded

step into our "Recovered Weapons
of Mass Destruction" room
where there's nothing at all
but a *Mission Accomplished* banner.
Replicas are for sale in our gift shop.

Drinking with Emmylou Harris

She never showed,
that one
from last night,
so
he slips coins
into the juke box
to drink instead
with Emmylou,
her voice
a kiss of hunger
and fire
as he orders
one
after
another –
scotch and
Emmylou
blurring
almost erasing
the empty
chair
beside
him.

50th Summer, 1998

My year old son can't wait any longer
to walk so he waddles across our lawn
like an intoxicated penguin, giggling
with the freedom of not needing

my hand and I feel such hesitant joy
watching him in this late summer sun
stumble toward all he's never known
on his own without me. Yesterday

a man shot two police, fathers
both, for no reason other than murder
and I ponder the world beyond our home
infected with violence in search of a target

and I shiver that my walking boy
assumes each stranger is just one more
person waiting to kiss him and love
his untamed hair, red as the ripe apples

that scent the air of my fiftieth summer.
But what lessons should I let happen
to my only child whose sneakered feet
lift like pistons in a tuned engine and make

me wish I could be his father and fifty
without the apprehension those years
have taught me. Someday he'll think
my caution is a clamp around his life

but now all he wants is to hurry across
our yard to the new sliding board
where I keep him at the top until
he pries my fingers loose to zigzag

all the way down. Then he staggers,
fists raised like Rocky, a self-propelling
champ in a diaper, headed now where
he needs to be. Something in his eyes
insists I get out of his way and let him go.

He Is Quitting School Today

Erik slumps at the guidance office table
with his textbooks to return and stares
at college posters like someone in a wheel chair
looking up at an escalator. His mother
fills out the blue "Withdrawal from School" form
on the opposite side of the room and I say, "Sorry,"
when she asks if she can smoke in here. Erik is 17,
his transcript smothered with F's and absences,
he sees no use in extending the emptiness
of warning notices for classes he's taken twice before.
Nothing I say this morning can change his mind.
He is quitting school today. His mother,
with the determined focus of a coroner, works
on the sheet writing the date of birth for the son
she once carried home from the hospital nestled
in a blue blanket and a parent's hope. Today
she leaves blank the space labeled, "Future Plans"
as Erik waits like a man in a midnight bus station
holding a ticket to nowhere.

To My Lifelong Friend Going to Prison

You said you thought the word was *pure*
to describe the moon light above us
the last night of our lives in boarding school
when you and I broke the rules and slept
outside under a blanket of young summer.
You had just written in my yearbook,
"We will always be this way, no secrets,
best friends, nothing will dim the gold
of what we had these years together."
And I, hopelessly in love with believing,
fell asleep with your words in my heart.

And years later your words were those
of blessing as you stood in sacred vestments
and placed your newly anointed hands
upon my head. You called upon Jesus
for me and I felt such grateful faith in you,
my friend, now a priest of God, now
a moral lighthouse ordained to show us
right from wrong. On Sundays I would envy
your hands as they held the host
and chalice in Catholic candlelight
as I knelt in worship and belief.

So now I don't know what to do,
old friend and molester of other fathers' sons.
On yesterday's front page you hid your face
with handcuffed hands like a convict,
like a coward, and I thought of those boys,
the horror their belief in you brought them,
their life sentence of limping through years
with memories of you. And I felt the chaos
of grieving what I had loved about you
as four decades of friendship crumbled
like an altar of ashes.

Michael, last night, your first in prison,
I dreamed you escaped to my back yard.
You were crying my name, sobbing
about forgiveness, begging me to remember
what we had been. But I stayed in the doorway,
my arms locked around my son,
a brother in innocence to the boys you damaged.
And when Liam asked me who you were
I stared out at your pleading eyes, your ugly
orange prison suit and told him, "Some criminal.
Stay close while I call the police."

Patriotism

*"The Pentagon has acknowledged
that Defense Secretary Donald Rumsfeld
did not sign condolence letters
to the families of soldiers killed in Iraq
but instead used a signature machine."*
The Washington Post, December 19, 2004

D-o-n-a-l-d R-u-m-s-f-e-l-d
that's 14 letters,
a lot to write,
takes effort
especially
that upper case "R"
I mean
it's not like writing an easy "L"
as in *Lincoln.*
He'd have to move his pen
down
go back up
make a loop
then move it
all the way
down again.
That takes work
and how much
can you ask
one man to give
up for his country?

In Peace Time, 1950

It was Mrs. Wilson's cat
Bill and Kenny drowned
in a puddle when they were five.
They held him in a vise
of baseball bats as he wiggled,
and, when the bubbles stopped,
Bill trembled with a strange arousal
before Mrs. Wilson came out screaming.

Bill's mother hated cats;
they made her sneeze. So he killed
to show he loved her, just as Andy,
his neighbor, bragged he loved America
as he'd down Budweisers
then repeat the best story on the street:
how he bayoneted a German in 1943.

But Bill's mother covered her mouth
when Mrs. Wilson phoned her
and when his father came home
he smacked his face so hard
Kenny swore he heard him
all the way down the block.
Bill was sent to bed without supper,
his parents said grace without him

while next door Andy slouched
on the porch stabbing beer after beer
with his army opener. He slurred
some drunken tune as Bill lay
in his bed picturing that German,
his stretched eyes pleading,
then Andy's blade shoving
through his uniform
and into his enemy heart.

Snakes

Perhaps it is the sound of the word,
that *snake* rhymes with *stake*
and hints of Dracula's ripped heart.
Or maybe the harsh "k" you find
in words like *kill* and *Ku Klux Klan*.
I feel a bit calmer with *reptile*,
that friendly long "I" and the "L"
from *smile* but that's only
wrapping razors in whipped cream.
It's no relief from those dead un-
blinking eyes or the corpse cold
of its hangman's rope body, no escaping
my stomach numbing fear
at the sight of them slithering, coiling,
their mouths wide as an opened grave,
venom waiting for fangs to find
the closest warm vein.

To Students Retrieving Gifts at a Crash Site Memorial for Friends Killed in a Drunk Driving Accident

You can take them home now.
Your friends lie somewhere else
beneath stones inscribed
with the small time of their lives.
Please take your teddy bears
with fur soft as gasoline smoke,
and your stuffed puppies
with their forever grins.
Gather the CD's
filled with their favorite songs
sweet as rum and coke, shrill
as screeching brakes, heavy with bass
pounding like a heart's last beat,
and wild as someone dancing after
his sixth whiskey. Pack these photos
of your friends skiing in air cold
as a beer keg, their faces red
as ambulance lights, take these candles
with flames trembling like parents
when the phone rings at 3 a.m.
And all your handwritten elegies,
such sober verses of loss,
take them with you. It is time
to speak your poems as prayers
and believe your friends can hear you.

Crossing in Fog

I hesitated
when Greg in a whisper begged me
to hold him. Greg, forsaken
by lover and family to suffer alone
the last lash of AIDS, asked for arms
around him and I remember
his breath, tiny as a baby's,
on my face when I lifted him
and squeezed death against my heart.

To cross a bridge in fog is to memorize fear
one step at a time, to believe in the danger
of life and water and the eternal
nothingness of one wrong turn.
To die in combat could be noble,
to die old among your children, beautiful.
But to die knowing those you love fear for their lives
leaves you only the clipboard care of masked strangers
in hospital white touching you with rubber gloves.

I left Greg early, my "appointment" a lie
I could live with as I rushed away
to the men's room for the scalding water
and stinging hand soap on my face.
In 231 a man who was my friend
would not see another summer,
would never know that I scrubbed my skin
raw, erasing all of him that I could,
my face red as shame in the fogging mirror.

III

Shifting Gears

In Case You Ever Wonder

for our son, Liam

It was a school night in September
and we were tired but love and need
drew us to each other when autumn's
first breath breezed our bedroom.
Afterwards, I held your mother
softly, like a flower ready to bloom,
and closed my eyes in the contented
sleep of the gratefully married.

Beneath my arms you began your miracle
of multiplication, one cell becoming
two, two cells becoming four, cells
upon cells, like dots in a Seurat portrait,
shaping into you, the son you will become,
the life we'll consider sacred as the soul
united with your name, blessed as the prayer
you have answered into our lives.

Liam and "The Wichita Lineman"

Liam wiggles like a terrified fish
when I lift him from his cradle at 3 a.m.,
his tears dot my pajama top and I
don't have a clue about what to do
to soothe him. So maybe it's some male-
bonding muse from the 60's that prompts me
to sing the soft loneliness of "The Wichita Lineman"
to my week old son who knows already
the pain of waking to nothing more
than the grin on his Big Bird night light.

I feel necessary as love here
in the dark of the nursery with Liam clinging
with frantic hands and, if I had words
he could understand, I'd tell him how good
it is to be a man and cry for someone.
But all I can do is whisper "The Wichita Lineman"
and hope a song about needing and wanting
for all time can ease him back to sleep. Then,
because it seems the right thing to do,
I begin to waltz with my son around the cradle

and his voice turns quiet as my slippers
on the carpet. I'm telling him about another man,
one of us, alone on a phone pole in Kansas,
whose hands clutch cable in the sky,
yearning perhaps for some of this peace
that grows within me dancing
with my newborn boy whose feet sway
like wires in the wind till he falls asleep
against my chest, his tiny breath a life
line wrapping around and around my heart.

The Other Mr. Romond

"Thank you," was all I could say when Shelby,
my 8th grade farm girl, raised her hand to tell me,
"Mr. Romond, I named a pig after you!"
And I could only answer, "Sure,"
when her family invited me over to meet
my namesake in person (or in pig) one Sunday
in spring when new flowers perfumed the air
except the air around the pig pen where
seven baby hogs busied themselves with the messy
task of being a pig. I nervously asked, "Which one
Is Mr. Romond ?" and Shelby carried over the ugliest
one of them all who smelled like Dr. Scholl's worst
nightmare. "You can pet him," urged Shelby and
I touched his head as if testing the texture
of a cow pie. But then he snorted and wiggled
his pink snout, his eyes widened with all
the affection a pig could give a non-pig and I swear
I heard him oink, "Hi, Mr. Romond. I love you!"
I gazed into his suddenly handsome countenance
as Shelby set him down and he waddled back
to his buddies with boring names like "Porky."
He spit and stomped slop upon the others as
I watched him with pride, a pig among pigs,
the other Mr. Romond, drooling, belching,
carrying on the family name.

Windowless Classroom

for Maggie Devine

You have to bring your own sun
when your classroom's designed
by one who must live in a shoe box.
Who else could ignore learning essentials
like light, and open windowed air
or the rapture of rain against glass ?
So it takes a special teacher
to bring the natural with her
into a room where light's measured
in watts, not beams, and air is processed
more than Velveeta cheese.
But kids know what is real
and kids learn with one
who is real, whose giving heart
casts a rainbow around synthetic
walls and opens the windows
of their souls by making autumn
winter and spring seasons of love
as she turns literature and writing
into personal suns and each morning
of each day this woman teaches
and lets the sunshine in.

Each Time the Curtain Rises

for Mia Zanette

So much they can show us in the dark.
The house lights die and then
a young voice acting older, the girl
from my lit class steps like a fawn
into the light and becomes another
and I believe her as I believe
the mystery of roses in my yard
growing red in a May midnight.

How I love what I feel watching
students create other lives
on stage, caring so much about lines
they've pressed into their minds.
My tongue becomes cotton
when they sing, my feet twitch
through each dance and my soul
glows when they do well
what they've rehearsed for months
of afternoons and evenings.

And I'd like them to know
I've felt that strange pain
in the thrill of a curtain call, that ache
when something beautiful is over. But
joy can stay on the stage of memory
and in an adult tomorrow, they can
close their eyes and live again
the night they turned paper scripts
into living theater, the miracle
that can happen behind school footlights
each time the curtain rises.

One

If I could have one
teaching moment
to live a second time,

just one piece
of an hour from 32 years
it would be that morning

at the end of third period
when a special needs
student waited until

all the others had left
to come up to my desk
holding with both hands

his copy of *Macbeth*
then with sunrise eyes
looked at me

and whispered,
"Mr. Romond,
I cannot believe

I am understanding this."

First Hair Cut

Liam sits on two phone books,
his head forward like a man
about to be knighted
as Joe the barber ever so slowly
snips his first hair that falls
like ribbons of copper velvet.
My son half squints and half
grins as Joe moves the scissors
with the care of a nervous surgeon,
slowly, so slowly as Liam's hair
splashes the floor in red
and I can't keep my eyes off my son,
his gorgeous, thick locks drifting
like maple leaves in October.
Then, in the mirror, I see my head
looking like a deceased cabbage, thinning
despair of a middle aged man who fears
high winds and photos from the back .

When it's my turn Joe surveys my skull
and announces, "This won't take long"
and races his scissors with all the care
of one snipping fuzz from a coconut.
I see my gray - brown strands joining
Liam's rich curls on the floor and I think
of how, like time, he has so much
of what I have so little. I pray my only child,
who waits coloring a bald Teletubbie,
has decades and decades of haircuts and love.
And someday, if some sweet girl glides
her fingers through his curls and whispers,
"Where'd you get such great hair?"
should he answer, "from my father,"
when she looks at me, may love
blind her enough to believe him.

Bald Spots

Like smashed baseballs they are almost circles
on our front lawn, 30 feet apart, beige exceptions
to the flawless grass around our house.
Two, sometimes three, sometimes four times a day
my son and I play catch, our sneakers erasing green
into these bald spots as we toss back and forth.
Eight year old Liam winds up and stings my glove
with a fast ball and talks of Randy Johnson but
I see Sandy Koufax and, like inverted mounds,
the spots sink farther into the earth, beautiful
as my father's tool handles polished smooth
by a life of hard work. We've thrown in rain,
we've thrown in darkness, once in March we
put on gloves under our gloves and threw in snow
and always to the soundtrack of our conversation,
a father and son's seeds for a garden of love
I pray will bloom all seasons. Today the *Chem Lawn*
man examines the twin blots marring the perfect green
and says, "Nothing will ever grow there"
and I want to answer, "You're wrong, Sir,"
as my son waits with his glove for another game
of catch, his feet ready to root even deeper
into our family ground.

Thanksgiving, 1958

It is the only day of the year
we eat in the dining room,
the only meal my mother
puts out her wedding china
and silver, the only time
we all dress up to eat
in our house on Albert St.
My father is not working
this Thursday and I do not
sit in 4th grade class with Sister Justin.
We are all smiling, the six of us,
Christmas catalogues arrive
tomorrow but I've already asked
for the rifle Chuck Connors fires
on *The Rifleman*. Since 5 a.m.
our house has smelled like turkey
and I know at age nine I love
this day, this time. Miles away
in Pennsylvania, Mary is living
her first week in the grateful awe
of her mother and father. Like lyrics
looking for music, we will not meet
for 23 years but my young life
has already taught me family love
and somewhere in my heart
I sense a blessing waiting for me,
someone precious to hold in years
beyond my fourth grade dreams.
So, as Mary breathes baby breath
in the Zanette family, we Romonds
bow our heads for grace and,
young as I am, I feel a truth
and a joy in thanking God
for all the present and future "gifts
which we are about to receive,"
my wife, days old, and our son, Liam,

39 years from our lives, busy
this Thanksgiving playing catch
with all of the angels.

Brother in Arms

for Charles H. Johnson

Everyone feared Mr. Stenner, even
the coarse fork truck drivers, Vietnam vets,
resentful of me, a college student
there for the summer. Peace marches,
draft card burnings were insults to their time
in Nam, sacrilegious to their buddies
who did not come home. But Mr. Stenner
was another story. He ruled the warehouse
without amnesty and, for unskilled men
with families to support, he held the artillery
of applications from other family men
desperate for a pay check. Time cards disappeared
for picking a wrong order or being late from lunch.
They would not look Mr. Stenner in the eye
and each day taught me how fear can cripple men
who had faced bombs and grenades on the other side
of the world. So it was, "Yes, Mr. Stenner,"
"Right away, Mr. Stenner" for they remembered
Tony who complained about loading a sweltering box car,
how the next day his locker was empty. I worked
among land mines avoiding Mr. Stenner and
the cold shoulders of vets who had no use for
a war protester with a deferment to major in English.
At lunch men wouldn't even look at me until the day
Mr. Stenner barged in and slapped my table
with an invoice screaming I had copied an 8 instead
of a 3 in the shipment code. He kept calling me
"retard" and "moron" and "idiot" until a voice said,
"Leave him alone." It was Max, six months back
from Saigon. Mr. Stenner walked slowly to his table
and stared into Max for what seemed eternity
but Max sat there clenching his thermos, staring right back
like a man who had learned to look death in the eye.
No one said a word after Mr. Stenner stormed out
to the shipping floor; everyone knew Max's wife

was expecting a baby. In a softer world the next scene
might have been Max and I embracing but he
ignored me and returned to his fork truck to find
his work order changed to loading a box car
all afternoon in air probably steaming to115 degrees.
At the whistle Max came in the locker room
his U.S. flag tattoo glistened his arm, his face blazed
with exhaustion. I tried to shake his hand but he brushed
past me, punched his card, and went to his car.
I drove out behind him knowing he had stepped
into the line of fire for me, not a friend, but a brother
in arms. Over and over I thanked him in my heart,
his red, white, and blue bumper sticker answered:
Vietnam vets – they fought for you.

Piano

It's only polished darkness in our living room
until Mary lets the music out.
I can't name one note of what she loves
and I've learned there's little
I can do to make her eyes light
as much as when she's touching the keys
into music. Sometimes on summer nights
I have seen neighbors stand in the street
listening to the music from her hands
and now, our young son sits on her lap
as she plays Beethoven around him.
I love the mystery of her fingers finding melody
where I see only black and white. I love her
smile as she follows the notes
for she knows how grateful I am
that, on my own, this Baldwin piano
would sing only silence but, because of her,
our home is filled with song.

Last Touch

for Mary and Liam

If it were up to me
I'd ask Death to wait
for an October Sunday
just after dusk
the seventh game
of the World Series
an hour away.
I'd make iced tea
the slow way, let it brew
till it was dark
as the inside of an urn
then I'd pour it
into souvenir mugs
we bought on the boardwalk.
I'd think about the sea,
the castle we built
how one of us cried at sunset
when waves taught us
the ache of letting go.
We'd sip tea with lemon
and sugar, share a red bowl
of popcorn and I'd be grateful
for it all: our family's pain
and sweetness, that love survived
these seasons and forgiveness
eased us into second chances.
I'd ask for one last dance
the three of us close,
the Beach Boys singing
"Warmth of the Sun" and
I'd beg Death to take me then,
before the music ended,
and let the last touch
of my life be your life
breath upon me,

something to keep
in the shadow of souls
where you'll find me
lonely with God
weeping both your names.

Catholic School May Crowning

All the other boys brought in crowns
from the florist, perfectly symmetrical,
exactly the same, but my mother made mine
with her own garden flowers. Each May
when Sister reached the "R's" and it was my turn
to bring a crown for a girl to place on Mary
my mother would step into the blooming spring
of our yard to snip lilacs, daisies, pink roses, and violets.
My mother, her apron a bouquet, carried them
into our kitchen to staple flower upon flower
onto a cardboard shirt collar till it bulged
with purple, pink, white and gold petals
blending like a family into a crown for Jesus' mother.
Next morning I'd carry it on a pillow behind a girl
who, that one day, was allowed to wear a dress
instead of a uniform. We'd walk the aisles of blue
jumpers and blue ties and blue suit coats as the class
sang, "Bring Flowers of the Fairest" till we reached
the front of the room. Then, as students began,
"O Mary We Crown Thee," the girl would need both hands
to lift my mother's crown onto Mary's head. And all day
through the numbing rote of catechism questions and answers,
the parched discourse of "Yes, Sister," "No, Sister," and
the row to row monotony of uniforms, blue as the Dead Sea,
there was Mary wearing a rainbow, blessed by my mother's hands,
overflowing with God's creations, no two of them the same.

Peanut Butter Cookies

My mother made them from memory
giving me my own memory of winter
in our kitchen, the salty aroma
of peanut butter cookies from the oven,
and the torture of waiting for them to cool
on the window sill overlooking Albert St.
in the Eisenhower 50's of my childhood.

I remember her mixing brown sugar,
butter, and spoons of Skippy. She never
checked a cookbook and they tasted
like no other cookies tasted. "I just know,"
she'd say if I asked her how she did this
then she'd wrap them in foil and sing
along with Perry Como on our radio.

They were as special as she was, a quiet
woman who took small joys in life
around the house. I know she knew
how much those cookies meant to me
for years later she apologized, as if
it were her fault, when a stroke at 80
erased the recipe from her mind.

So she followed a Betty Crocker recipe
and the cookies were tasty and fine
but lacked the magic of what she had lost.
I swore they were as good as the ones
she used to make but I was hiding my hunger
for her own peanut butter cookies, hiding
my fear of the first taste of good-bye.

Believing like a Child

At three my son hasn't learned
how to doubt. He believes
what he believes so I am
speechless when he points
at a picture of my mother,
deceased nine years, and says,
"This is the nice old lady
who visits me sometime
when I am sleeping."
He says she kisses him,
combs his red hair
with her fingers and whispers
she loves him. She only
speaks in whispers, he says.
His face is calm, matter of fact,
as if he's asking
for jelly on a cracker.
Do I break his faith and tell him
my mother's loving
sweetness will always be
missing for him, that her love
was subtracted from his life
before he ever came to be?
Could my own loneliness
for my mother and tortured
yearning for her to see
her grandson somehow
have nudged his imagination
and turned wish into apparition?
I say nothing, close the photo
album and button his pajamas
before carrying him up to bed
where he sleeps, his arms spread
like an angel. I look at his face
and think of what he told me
and my heart begins racing

———

ahead of my mind. Could it be
there really is a God so kind
he would open death's door
for my mother to see my only child
in this world? *But this is crazy.*
I am thinking; *this is beautiful*
I am feeling as I linger
in my son's room wondering
where dreams may take him tonight.
Will he hear a tender voice
giving him family love?
Will hands that once held me
now ruffle his soft curls? I remain
by his side and begin to pray
for the impossible, believing
like a child, whispering
into the mortal darkness.

Painting

One Saturday
when I was ten my father,
a truck driver, taught me
how to paint using our porch
steps as his classroom.
I can still feel his huge hand
around mine guiding the brush
brilliant with green paint
across the wooden step
and the thrill of watching
the pigment sink in, turning
scuffed to glossy. My father
told me, "Always bring the
brush back into where you
have just painted, before
you go on to the new spot,"
and he would move my hand
to the left then slide the brush
onto the next patch of worn wood.
We painted two steps together
then he let go of my hand and
honored me by letting me paint
the bottom step on my own.
I still hear his voice urging
me to bring the brush back
to blend the paint into one
continuous stroke of green.
I don't know why after 50 years
these words remain
like lyrics of a favorite song
but I keep seeing that Saturday,
and feel the paint on my fingers
and hear my father's soft
instruction as I now bend to
my young son and guide his hand
holding a paint brush across

his skate board ramp. I repeat
the exact words of my father
and hear him speaking with me
then feel his hand upon my hand
holding his grandson's hand
as together we guide Liam's brush
across the ramp, reaching back
to go forward, our brush marks red
as a bloodline, seamless, beautiful.

Strength

Liam has asked to wear his suit.
Only the second time in his life
he is putting on the tailored pants
and pinstriped, three button jacket.
He searches his drawer for his one
pair of dress socks, he finds his polished
oxfords in the back corner of his closet.
I see nervousness, no, I see fear in his eyes
as I knot his tie and slide it up his white shirt
ironed for a morning we will all remember.
"You don't have to do this," I tell him,
"there are others Mommy and I can ask."
But he looks at me with that same scared
but determined look I saw seven years ago
on his first day of school. "No, Daddy,
I am going to do this." "You're only 12,"
I answer, "the others are grown men.
No one will blame you if you change your mind."
And he repeats, "No … I am going to do this."
And hours later I am watching him
use both hands to do what the five men
around him do with one and I am struck
by how much I envy my own son and
wonder if I could have done when I was 12
what he is doing now as he walks sideways
over the cemetery snow giving all
his strength to gripping the gold handle
on his grandfather's casket as we follow
in his foot prints, our eyes blurred
with sorrow and pride.

Shifting Gears

The time it takes to snap my fingers
seems longer than the years
since I first held my son
on a bicycle then watched
him make his world a little larger
pedaling down our street and disappearing
onto the next before returning
with a Lindbergh grin to our driveway.
It all seems less than a breath
ago as I watch him now at age 11
commandeer his roaring dirt bike,
80 cc's of galloping Honda power
shifting from first to fourth,
rocketing up, down, and around
the hills, his smile the smile
of one born for propulsion,
who could not be more different
from his father who thinks twice
before taking an escalator.
He screeches to a stop and asks
if he can give me a ride
and my love blinds my fear
as I get on the back, my old bones
and butt already feeling each lump
and bump on the motorcycle trails.
How quickly it has come to this
shifting of gears that I, his father,
depend upon my son for safe passage,
that I now trust him as he trusted me
to steer through all the twists and turns.
I put my arms around his waist as he revs
the engine, lets out the clutch and shouts
over his shoulder, "Hold on to me, Dad!"
And I do.

About the Author

Edwin Romond's book *Dream Teaching* (Grayson Books, 2005) has gone through multiple printings. His work has appeared in journals such as *The Sun, Tiferet, The Pittsburgh Quarterly, Lips, Zone 3, Poet Lore, New Letters, Barrow Street, The Rockhurst Review*, as well as in college texts and anthologies. He has been awarded poetry fellowships from the National Endowment for the Arts, and from both the New Jersey and Pennsylvania State Councils on the Arts.

Romond was a public school teacher for 32 years in Wisconsin and New Jersey before retiring. He lives in Wind Gap, Pennsylvania with his wife, Mary, and their son, Liam.

Acknowledgements

Grateful acknowledgment is made to the editors of these journals in which the following poems, some in slightly different versions, previously appeared:

Art of Music Anthology, "Liam and the Wichita Lineman," "Piano"

Barrow Street, "For the Movie of My Life I Audition Former Lovers for the Part of Muse"

Coal City Review, "After 11 Years"

Edison Review, "Almost Forever," "The Other Mr. Romond"

Exit 13, "Bald Spots," "Catholic School May Crowning"

Empty Mirror Arts Magazine, "Patriotism"

Journal of New Jersey Poets, "Driving Home from Knoebels Amusement Park," "My Request of Yankee Stadium Demolition Workers

Lake Effect, "Johnny Cash"

Lips, "Divorced Parents at a Little League Game," "My Mother at 20," "Peanut Butter Cookies," "Shifting Gears,"

Loch Raven, "Green."

NJCTE English Journal, "Each Time the Curtain Rises," "He Is Quitting School,"

Paterson Community College Literary Journal, "In Peace Time, 1950"

Sun Magazine, "Alone with Love Songs," "Brother in Arms," "Last Touch," "To My Lifelong Friend Going to Prison"

Think Journal, "50th Summer"

Tiferet, "Believing like a Child"

U.S. 1 Work Sheets, "Night Watchmen"

Verse Wisconsin, "Painting"

Voices from Here, "First Hair-Cut,"

Words on the Wall, "Decembers"

"To My Lifelong Friend Going to Prison" won First Place in the 2005 Fanny Wood Poetry Competition.

"Drinking with Emmylou Harris" won First Place in the 2009 *Art of Music* Poetry Contest.

"Alone with Love Songs" also appears in *The Mysterious Life of the Heart*, Sun Publishing Co. 2009.

"Last Touch" also appears in *Star Child*, Jennifer J. Martin, iUniverse Publishing Co., 2006.

Thank you to my wife, Mary, and to our son, Liam, for their love and support. Much gratitude also to Ginny Connors at Grayson Books for her help in editing this book.